Terms and Conditions

LEGAL NOTICE

The Publisher has strived to be as accurate and complete as possible in the creation of this report, notwithstanding the fact that he does not warrant or represent at any time that the contents within are accurate due to the rapidly changing nature of the Internet.

While all attempts have been made to verify information provided in this publication, the Publisher assumes no responsibility for errors, omissions, or contrary interpretation of the subject matter herein. Any perceived slights of specific persons, peoples, or organizations are unintentional.

In practical advice books, like anything else in life, there are no guarantees of income made. Readers are cautioned to reply on their own judgment about their individual circumstances to act accordingly.

This book is not intended for use as a source of legal, business, accounting or financial advice. All readers are advised to seek services of competent professionals in legal, business, accounting and finance fields.

You are encouraged to print this book for easy reading.

Table Of Contents

Foreword

Chapter 1:
Blogging Basics

Chapter 2:
How Important Is Design

Chapter 3:
Provide Sought After Content And Keywords

Chapter 4:
Hold A Contest

Chapter 5:
Use Social Media

Chapter 6:
Use Video

Chapter 7:
Use Audio And Podcasts

Chapter 8:
Use Well Know Guest Bloggers

Chapter 9:
Build Backlinks

Chapter 10:
Using Comments

Wrapping Up

Foreword

I tools available through the internet platform communication that is rapidly gaining momentum in its vast and unbridled usage. Through the blogging platform information can be shared, viewed, commented upon and discussed. Get everything you need to know here.

Achieve Blogging Buzz
Insider Info On How To Have Your Blog On Everyone's Lips

Chapter 1:
Blogging Basics

Synopsis

Blogging can be an effective way to get the important recognition needed for the success of any business endeavor. Using the blogging tool to create a "buzz" can an usually does elevate the business position to a more visible level and this of course can in turn act positively towards creating an effective advertising campaign for the said endeavor. Such campaigns if done on a positive note can be both very helpful and also cost effective.

The Basics

Ideally the individual's blog should be designed to reflect the niche it intends to cater to as effectively and informatively as possible while all the time maintaining the element of attention grabbing and be current.

It should also be user friendly. This important fact should not be over looked as many blogs which are not user friendly will end up becoming redundant and thus defeating its purpose in getting the content noticed. Choosing a platform and blog name that is going to get the attention of the intended target audience also has its merits.

Though still considered a little controversial in its delivery and designed content make up the blog is also popularly used as an advertising tool for sponsored posts.

These usually get posted in the form of feedback, reviews, opinions, videos and many other avenues that are created through the information passed between parties with some level of vested interest.

Chapter 2:
How Important Is Design

Synopsis

Although providing and sourcing information is an important fact linked to the existence of the internet, there is a certain level of consideration that should be given as to how this information is going to come across to the eventual interested party. Designing the information to get and hold the interest of the viewer is very important to its success and blogging is no exception.

How it Looks

Blogging predominantly offers those on line a way to interact both of a personal level as well as on a business platform level. The blogging exercise has proven its merits over time and is now considered a very effective tool indeed that is often accepted as a good avenue to get a site traffic driven.

This potential money making tool needs to follow some tried and true methods to stay competitive and relevant as this is the only way it is going to sustain its popularity status.

Well designed sites will the factor that keeps the visitors coming back for more. A fresh and attention grabbing look will give the viewer something to think about and thus create the attraction to get the interaction exercise going.

The following are some tips to ensuring the best points are included to make a well designed blog page:

- Customize the header to ensure it does not look generic. The idea is to be able to stand out from the very onset of the design. Getting professional help is fine but not necessary as with a little thought and some research a suitable header can be designed.

- Using photos is also another good idea as the visual effects it will provide can be both eye catching and informative at the same time. Most people today are more in tuned with the visual effects of information rather than the actual written matter.

- Including a RSS feed is also beneficial as it will facilitate the following experience to be easier and ensure those interested can keep themselves updated and informed.

Chapter 3:
Provide Sought After Content And Keywords

Synopsis

In order to design a blog that is going to be able to draw the desired amount of traffic the individual is going to have to put in some time researching the wants and needs of the intended target audience. Then armed with this information the design phase of the blog can commence using suitable content and attention grabbing keywords.

The Material

Increased traffic to the site will ideally translate to possible positive revenue for the individual and thus creating a viable business platform.

Keywords are the tools that help to ensure the visitor is directed to the site with the help of the said words they would key into their respective searches. This will then allow them to view the contents which should be all accounts be relevant to the keywords chosen.

Besides this the keywords also provide an insight to the positioning of the competitors success rates of failures and allows the individual to better position themselves to avoid the pit falls of others.

The relationship of the search engines with the traffic directions to any particular blog or site also lies in the choice of the keywords used in both the title and the content of the site.

These keywords will direct the traffic to the site through the tools provided when the corresponding word or words appear or connect to the prospects' search.

Using tools to gauge the attraction features of any particular word or phrase intended to be used for keyword traffic directing purposes is also another way to gauge the potentially good keyword choices.

Suitable and relevant content matter is also equally important to consider when compiling information for the blog. If the information feature is out of date or not in any way connective to the subject matter the title suggests the blog is in danger of being blacklisted or worse struck off.

Chapter 4:

Hold A Contest

Synopsis

Using different ways and means to attract traffic to a particular blog or site is the most important reason and desired effect most exercises are designed around. An innovative way of ensuring traffic is directed to a blog is to organize a contest.

Grab Attention

Contests are a great way to draw attention to a blog especially is the contest elements are exciting on every level. The interaction created by the draw to the contest can be hugely beneficial to the site.

However the contest should be well thought up and designed to ensure the visitor is not a touch and run interested party who either does not have the time to commit to the cause behind the contest or has no interest in doing so.

The contest should ideally be designed to get the prospect to be interactive to the extent of being able to completely identify with the product at least midway thought the exercise.

The following are some reasons to consider including contests are part of the blog content:

- The most potent form of marketing is through word of mouth and this can be achieved through the posting of contests whereby the viewing target audience can be increased by leaps and bounds to an infinite amount.

- The engagement of the target audience can be readily facilitated through the launching of any well designed contests. This will then create the multiple exchange

channels that will eventually generate the valuable; interaction of a wider basis.

- The reward incentives offered by complete participation from the visitor logged onto the blog will have to be done in a manner that is worthwhile to the individual. Most visitors will be reluctant to participate beyond certain levels and in order to ensure optimized participation the contest rewards have to be well worth the effort.

Chapter 5:
Use Social Media

Synopsis

The use of social media as a tool for increasing traffic to a blog or site will eventually ideally lead to better exposure for the business entity and eventual better revenue earning for that business entity.

Social Sites

Blogging is a way to get the product or service noticed on the social media platform when there is constant interaction and the exchange of material related to the elements in the blog space.

The high amount of commenting and exchange of events or product information generated can usually create enough of "buzz" to keep the blog in the forefront of interest. It is also a great way to give interested parties an insight into the varied perspectives of the entity being touted.

As a marketing strategy it is an excellent way to use the social media to drive traffic to the site as blogging has fast gained a strong foothold in the arena of internet activity.

This form of garnering widespread methods of communicating has lead to the successful expansion of any site where blogging is fundamentally featured as the strongest traffic pulling tool.

A lot of individuals today choose to actively participate in the "advertising" engine of their product or business thereby ideally creating the interaction though blogging.

Developing the habit to always design high content that is rich in relevant and helpful information is what the social media scene is always on the lookout for, thus being able to present this adequately though the blog process is beneficial on so many different levels.

The branding positioning done through the social media via blogging is also another reason to consider this option. The constant exchange of information that is favorable in nature will eventually ensure the exposure of the blog or site to its optimum levels thus creating the desired traffic draw to the site with the impressive revenue returns.

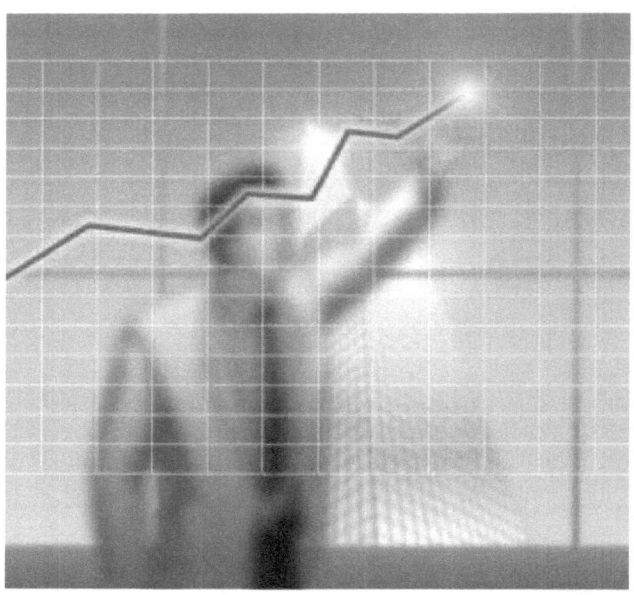

Chapter 6:
Use Video

Synopsis

Capitalizing on the various on line tools to generate the desired traffic to the site to create the access to possible revenue should be explored to its maximum capacity possible. In doing so one may come across the recommended use of the video tool for blogging.

Sight

Below are some of the reasons why one should seriously consider using video for enhancing the blogging experience:

- If the idea is to set one's work apart from the rest in order to gain the element of surprise and interest then blogging using video based information would prove to be beneficial and definitely fit the requirements above. A lot of people today prefer to explore this further as it helps to ensure the eventual makeup of the page is interesting and exciting with the help of the video.

- There is a whole different segment of viewer on the internet platform who would prefer to get information through visual aids like video rather than the more conventional way of the written word. Thus by using video one is able to tap into this segment of users quite successfully.

- Video also explains things better as it is done in demonstrative manner where the viewer get to immediately view the information and corresponding results as opposed to trying to figure it out through the write up given.

There are several different online platforms that use the video style messaging and this of course has its own set of target audience which

caters to a much wider range of interested parties. These various other marketing platforms can then assist in garnering new traffic generation opportunities.

However it should also be noted that for some the process of creating a video can be quite challenging and thus may prove to be a choice not well made. Therefore before attempting to use the video style to facilitate traffic growth, one should first consider all the processes that go into making one.

Chapter 7:
Use Audio And Podcasts

Synopsis

Before deciding on the type of online marketing tool to use, one should first consider the target audience possible preferences. If the target audience intended is not very computer savvy then the choice of tools made should also be able to cater effectively to this segment of viewers. Using audio and podcast may provide an interesting way of accessing information provided the user is knowledgeable enough to do so.

Sound

Some of the advantages that would be clear when using the audio and podcast facility would be as follows:

- Being a form of background media the audio tool does require a lot less manipulation than other forms of media tools available.
- The audio process generally takes a lot less time and effort when compared to other more demanding tools. This cut in production time also constitute to a lesser budget needed, thus making it a good option to choose.
- The audio tool also required less bandwidth which is another very beneficial aspect.
- The formats and compressions are also a lot easier to understand and eventually implement or use when compared to other tools.

Studies have shown that a viewer is more likely to browse through a podcast which contain a lot of information but formatted in an interesting and attention grabbing fashion as compared to a much shorter mental commitment to other tools.

This then facilitates the convening of more information thus benefiting the possibility of better revenue through the buying of items being touted.

Mainly due to its feature of being accessible the podcasting audio content is very much sought after. The RRS feed makes it an easily accessible feature which also facilitated the accessing period on demand. This is suitable as it allows the individual to dictate where and when to access the information featured.

Chapter 8:
Use Well Know Guest Bloggers

Synopsis

Getting the highest amount of traffic to a site should be the priority when it comes to picking the most suitable internet complimenting tools. Using guest bloggers is just another recommended way to ensure this ideal situation surfaces.

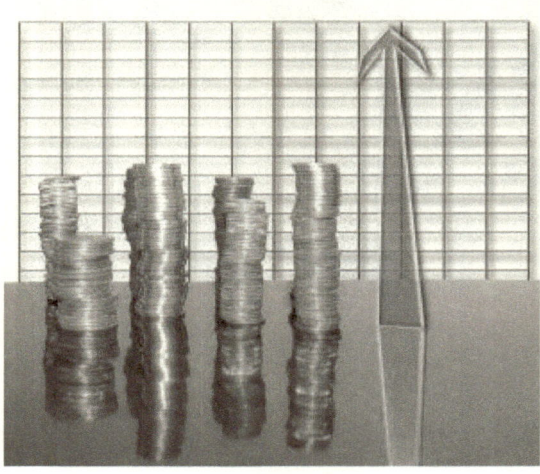

Keep Them Coming Back

The following are some reasons why one should consider guest bloggers for the purpose of optimizing traffic to a site:

Getting the required amount of traffic with the intention of generating profit is not always possible through the random use of internet marketing tools.

However this does not really apply to the guest blogger tool where it is intentionally able to draw the quality traffic that is needed for the purpose of definitely ensuring a higher probable percentage of purchasing viewers.

Using guest bloggers to successfully build authoritative backlinks to a particular blog site is one way of generating more traffic. With the help it contributes to building the domain name and search engine authority this tool is both needed and very effective indeed.

Creating an impact that has a high level of influence is also another reason guest bloggers are almost always a welcome addition to a site. The opinions posted at some of the site by the guest blogger can make or break a business campaign.

Therefore having this tool if it is done is a positive light then the advertising angle it is perceived to have is rather powerful indeed.

The influence some of the guest bloggers have is phenomenally wide and convincing. Featuring guest bloggers who have a substantial portfolio of their own can be viewed as impressive and credible thus ensuring the information posted is sought after.

Being associated with other top guest bloggers will also eventually lend a certain amount of credibility to the individual's own blog. Thus making the effort to build a level of authority in any particular field to facilitate this alliance could prove to be beneficial.

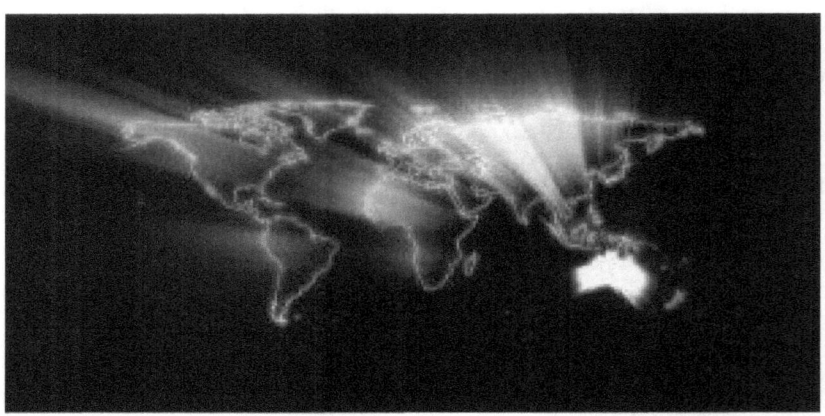

Chapter 9:
Build Backlinks

Synopsis

Building backlinks is one way of doing this as it requires more work from the other parties rather that from the individual itself.

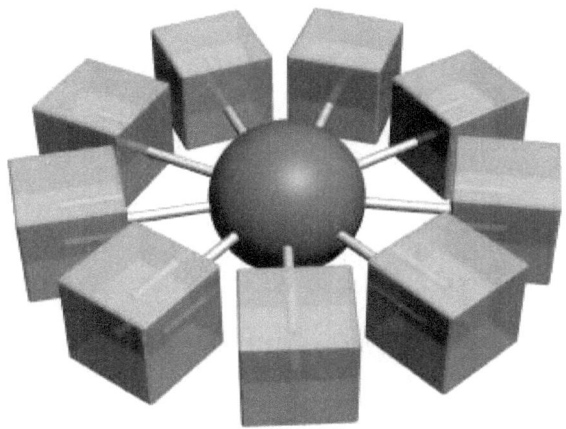

Building Links

Crucial to the success of SEO optimization the backlinks will eventually provide for the increased amount of traffic which will ideally generate revenue through the blogging platform.

Although the host often does not have control or commenting power on the actual exercise of developing and designing the contents of the site the mere fact that the backlinks have been accepted and established will create some level of similarity which the viewer is looking for when they click on the link.

Using backlinks to enhance the preexisting original site will help provide information from other sources and perhaps even other connective information that would be very useful to the viewer clicking on the backlinks.

This can also work in favor of the host which may have credible and interesting information that may be sourced by other interested parties to be added as backlinks to their sites too.

Getting listed in directories, posting in forums, other blogs and article directories will eventually facilitate for the ideal backlinks process. Some sites often look towards backlinks to provide more information to compliment the already existing featured at the host site.

In choosing to use backlinks there are also some important points that one needs to consider in order to lessen the possibility of negative impacts. One of the negatives would include the use of links exchanges. This method of barter links may be good in some ways but is often abused thus causing more problems than being a helpful element.

Chapter 10:
Using Comments

Synopsis

Commenting on blog posting can be an added advantage to tap into when trying establishing a wider audience for the business, product or service being promoted. Using this tool should ideally be able to facilitate more interactive participation to the site thus causing the curiosity element to emerge for those wanting to get the latest on the information posted.

The Comments

The following are some convincing reasons why the use of comments should be considered to enhance the position of a blog:

The regular exercise of commenting on blogs will create the opportunity for the building of contacts and leads to more connections and maybe even the invitation to being part of guest blogging on sites. It can also constitute to the establishment of new business opportunities.

Commenting on a regular and informative fashion can also help to raise the profile of the individual's position in a particular area as through the avenue of getting noticed the element of popularity may be created.

Posting regular comments can also help to drive traffic to the individual's own blog as here again those following the comments will definitely want to also visit and be privy to the commentator's material.

Commentating can also be a form of getting involved in a debative form of information exchange. This will give rise to the element of excitement where the exchanging of information becomes proactive and also of being able learn a thing or two.

Sparking newer and more innovative ideas can also be part of the positive product output of any commenting exercise. The ideas can come from the comment exchange exercise where more heads are put together to cause the positive exchange of ideas to create new elements. This is a great way to invent new thought processes as the commenting can take on a very benefit driven endeavor.

Wrapping Up

Some sources strongly believe the relevance of a blog is placed at great risk in terms of credibility when it facilitates commercial activity. This however has not stopped the blogging platform from gaining popularity as an important and relevant avenue for getting recognized for better or for worse.

www.ingramcontent.com/pod-product-compliance
Lightning Source LLC
Chambersburg PA
CBHW030546220526
45463CB00007B/3004